I Love my Kinky Hair!

Written by Nadene McKenzie-Reid

Illustrated by Carlee Reid

Edited by Tena-Lesly Reid

Library of Congress Control Number: 2016906292

ISBN-10: 0692634150
ISBN-13: 978-0692634158

DEDICATION

To all the moms that had to have the "Kinky Hair" conversation and all the girls who sat through the grooming without realizing just how beautiful they really were.

My Mom said, "Carlee, time to wash your hair!"

"Oh no!" I thought with panic and fear.

Hair Days are the worst for me,

As my hair is anything but tangle free.

My hair is so thick and kinky.

Why couldn't it be blonde and silky?

I ask my mom to let it out.

She always says no and I pout.

"But my friends have their hair out all the time!"

How could my mom be so unkind?

"Your hair is different," she replied.

But she saw the sadness in my eyes.

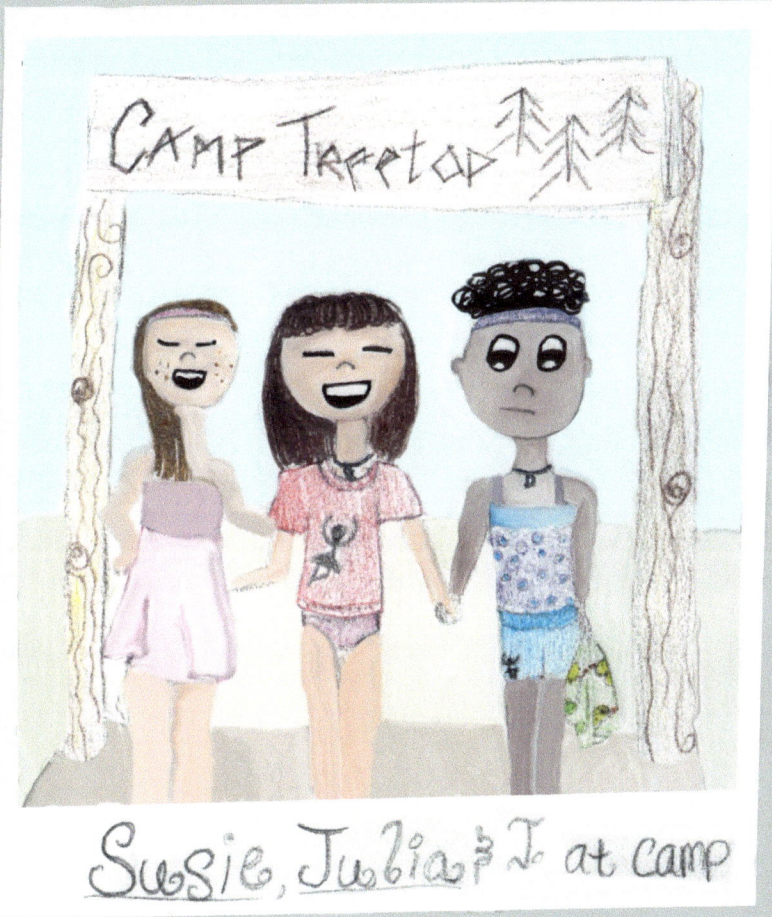

Camp Treetop

Susie, Julia & I at camp

"Different is still pretty," she said.

As she combed the mop upon my head.

2014 MOST
BEAUTIFUL!

"It's hard feeling different Mom, I just want to blend in."

"But I have different hair and different skin."

"I walk through school and feel like kids stare.

Things would be different if I changed my hair!"

"I use a cap to cover my head.

I walk the hallways with sorrow and dread!"

Mom sighed, "Real friends aren't made by your looks,

But from common interests like hobbies and books."

"They should see you for the beauty you are inside,

So be true to yourself and don't you dare hide."

Kindergarten Frens

"You got your hair from God," Mom said,

As the comb broke when she tugged on my head.

"Don't mind if it can't lay flat,

Or takes long to oil and plait."

"Your hair and skin are a package deal.

  With them, your roots are revealed."

"Don't curse your hair or be ashamed,

  Because your forefathers would have fought in vain."

"That hair was on our Olympic gymnastics sensation,

As she brought home gold for our nation."

"She made history and it was clear,

There is more to people than just hair."

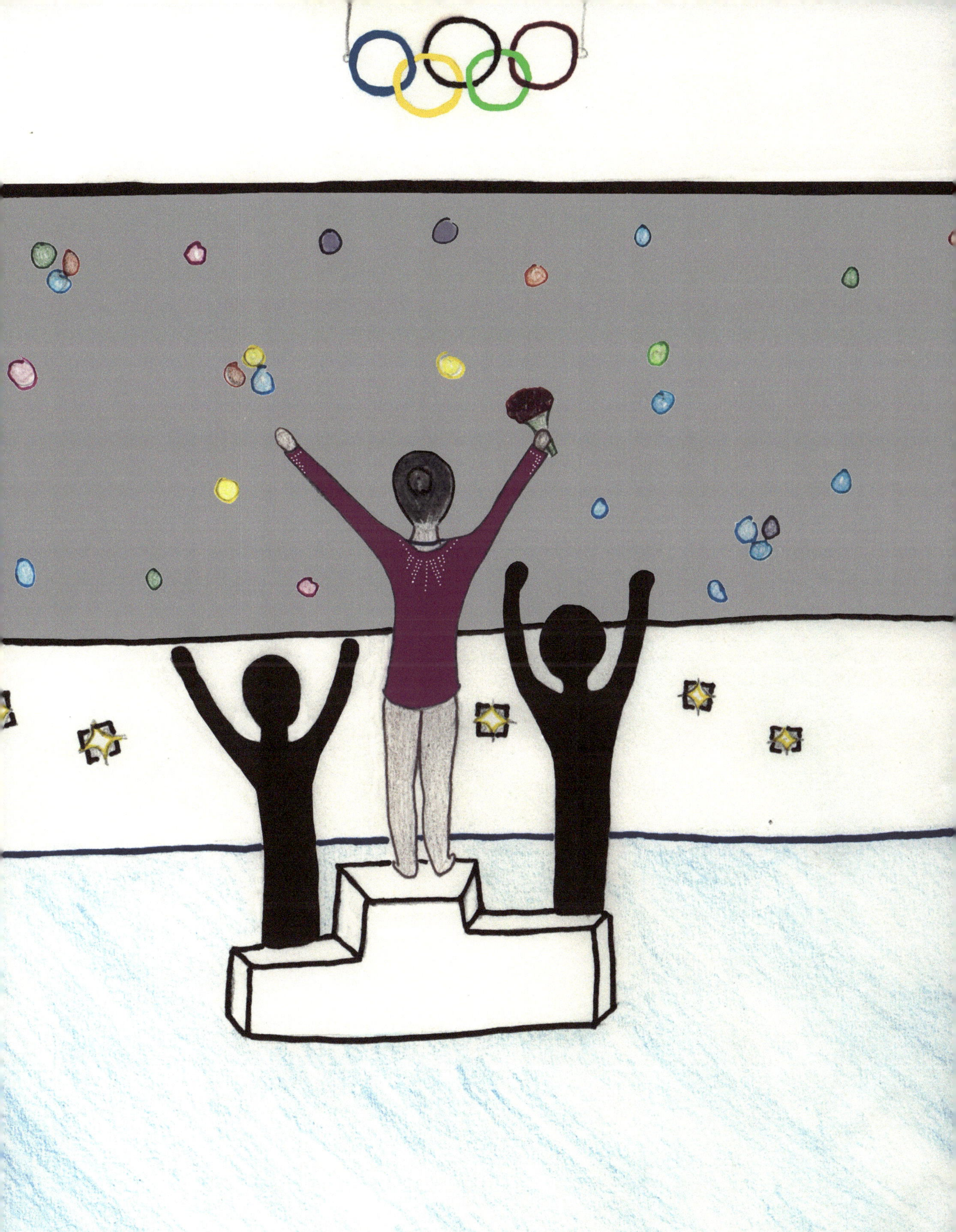

"You can make it a problem if you so choose,

But in the end, it is you that will lose."

"So be happy and proud of who you are,

My little Kinky-haired star."

"You were beautiful from the start,

Because of your good, kind heart."

I looked in the mirror and what did I see?

Beautiful cornrows ended with beads.

As I shook my head from left to right,

I couldn't help but admire the sight.

I am beautiful, what my mom said is true,

Because real beauty starts inside of you.

So gone are my hang-ups and despair.

Because now, I LOVE my kinky hair.

ABOUT THE AUTHOR

At first glance, this book will easily resonate with anyone dealing with washing a black girl's hair. But my goal is for it to reach beyond that. It is to share a perspective that I feel very few people are aware of.

I am not a professional writer. I am a working mom, born in Jamaica and raising two girls and a boy with my husband in America. What is the relevance you might wonder? Well unbeknownst to us, our upbringing in Jamaica didn't prepare us completely for raising our kids in America. We both migrated post-adolescence to the U.S. with a rich culture, identity and sense of self. I was naïve enough to think that these were inborn or at the very least transferable traits. Traits that I would pass on to my kids effortlessly. Imagine my surprise when each of my kids at various stages, approached me about being "different", wanting to change physical attributes and not feeling as though they were on a level playing field. My theory had been ripped to shreds.

I started to look around for books catering to children having these issues but never found any that addressed the matter the way I wanted it to. So I decided to write books that addressed these issues that my kids had raised to me. I decided to start with the hair. Then I procrastinated. I tucked my story in a drawer and left it there for a while. When the Gabby Douglas Olympic Hair criticism made headline news, I knew it was time to revisit the drawer. I decided I was going to proactively pursue getting this book published. I felt compelled to share my stories so little children of color can get a head start on confidence, so they can achieve their true potential.

ABOUT THE ILLUSTRATOR

My name is Carlee and I am 12 years old at the time this book is being published. I enjoy drawing, reading, playing the violin and last but not least, gymnastics. I had just turned 11 years old when I illustrated this book my mom wrote that is based on my experiences and feelings around the time I was 7. I trust you will find her words as comforting and reassuring as I did. I hope you enjoy our labor of self love.

www.ingramcontent.com/pod-product-compliance
Lightning Source LLC
Chambersburg PA
CBHW041223040426
42443CB00002B/62